DAVID ROBERTS

A journey in Egypt

Commentary on drawings by David Roberts: Rita Bianucci

INTRODUCTION

David Roberts was neither the first nor the only artist to travel in the Middle East bringing back drawings of the places and peoples he had seen, but he is certainly the most famous. He was born in Edinburgh in 1796 into a humble family. His father was a cobbler, and he himself started to work at a very young age. By the time he was eight he was already a painter, specialised in the imitation of marble and wood. Even after he obtained a post as a scene-painter in Scotland he continued to practice his old trade in the periods in which the theatre did not require his work. Subsequently, he was employed full time in the theatres of Glasgow, Edinburgh and, from 1822, London, where he worked for the famous opera-house at Covent Garden. At the same time Roberts started to exhibit water-colours and oil-paintings, as well as illustrating books with his sketches, gaining praise from the critics and enjoying fair commercial success.

In the years from 1824 to 1830, he travelled in France, Belgium, Holland and Germany. In 1832-33 he spent 11 months in Spain, visiting the north, Madrid, and then proceeding down to Granada, Cordova and Gibraltar. From there he crossed over to Marocco, leaving the European continent for the first time. He then visited Seville, remaining there for five months.

During his stay abroad he produced drawings and oil paintings, and once back home, he illustrated four issues of "The Landscape Annual" and published 27 lithographic prints in "Roberts' Picturesque Sketches of Spain".

His work was well received and the numerous Spanish subjects that he produced in the following years were sold with no difficulty. With the money earned in this way he organised his tour in the East.

Thus, in 1838-9, he spent 11 months travelling in Egypt, Syria and the Holy Land.

After his return home, he was elected as a member of the Royal Academy (1841) and the year after, he started to publish the drawings made during his tour, monthly, in collaboration with the lithographer Louis Haghe. These drawings made him famous in Britain and elsewhere.

In 1843, he was once again travelling through Europe and ten years later (1853-54) he spent six months in Rome and Naples. When he died, on the 25th November 1864, the humble painter was a famous man whose customers were rich businessmen and noblemen; even Queen Victoria and Prince Albert commissioned work from him and he himself visited the court on several occasions in order to discuss it. Roberts' fame is due to his ability in architectural drawings and those of monuments, but he also painted scenes from daily life. He was fascinated by the ruins left by men of past ages and returned many times to the same place, drawing his subject from various view points and at different hours, taking care to catch the variations in the light at different moments in the day. His works provide a precise, almost photographic, documentation of the appearance of ancient Egypt, now forever lost.

Alexandria, commonly called Cleopatra's Needle

Alexandria: "Cleopatra's Needles"... - *These obelisks have been called "Cleopatra's Needles" since the Middle Ages, even though they are in no way connected with the Egyptian queen. According to Pliny they stood before the Caesareum, the sanctuary in honour of the deified Emperor, which was started by Cleopatra and finished by Augustus.*
The obelisks had originally been erected by Tuthmosis III on the occasion of the third jubilee of his reign to honour his "father" Re-Harakhty in Heliopolis, the seat of some of the most important religious organizations in the country. The ovals on the sides of the obelisks bear the names of Tuthmosis III and of the later Ramesses II, called the Great. They were transported to Alexandria in 10 BC by Augustus.
When Roberts arrived in Alexandria this is how he saw the two monolyths, as the earthquake of 1301 had left them: still intact, even though one had fallen.
The almost hazy appearance of the surrounding ruins backed by the glittering expanse of the sea contribute to create the atmosphere which envelops the monuments: an atmosphere of desolate decay, but at the same time of the proud affirmation of a past which defies death.

... and the "Pillar of Pompey" - *The "Pillar of Pompey", made of red granite from Aswan like "Cleopatra's needles", is situated on high ground which allows it to stand out against the surrounding countryside. Its name, dating from the time of the Crusades, derives from it being erroneously believed to be the cenotaph of the general who was killed on Egyptian soil. In actual fact the pillar was part of the Serapeum, the Ptolemaic temple dedicated to the god Sarapis.*
The foundations are made up of elements from much older monuments, as is testified for example by the name of Sethos I carved on one of the blocks. The capital is Corinthian and, as the hollow on top of it suggests, was probably intended to hold a statue.
An inscription on the pedestal informs us that the monument was re-erected in 292 AD by Publius, the Roman Prefect of Egypt, in honour of the Emperor Diocletian.
In the nineteenth century, the pillar was still a reference point for sailors, and travellers coming from the desert due to its high position and its size.

Cairo: the market - On visiting Cairo, Roberts could not help but feel the fascination that the Eastern world holds for travellers: the scenes from daily life which are so different from the West, the slave market, Islamic architecture; all this made just as great an impression on Roberts as the monuments of ancient Egypt. The market, with its colours, with its pungent smells, with the people lingering in front of this or that stall to appraise the wares or to bargain endlessly over prices, had always been and still is, a picturesque and compulsory stop for tourists.

Giza - Nineteenth century travellers could easily reach the zone of the pyramids if the level of the Nile was low and the intersecting canals dry and practicable: it took little more than an hour to journey from New to Old Cairo, cross the Nile on the ferry and finally reach the the village of Giza, from which the most famous group of pyramids in the world takes its name.
The journey became tortuous and much longer if the Nile was in flood and travel through the canals was no longer possible.
The pyramids looked like this to Roberts from the East bank of the river: immense, despite their distance from the river, perfect forms rising out of the sands of the Libyan desert and projected into the sky. In front is the pyramid of Cheops, then that of Chephren, and lastly the pyramid of Mycerinus, all dating back to the Fourth Dynasty. Moved by the sight of them, the artist wrote: "What are the portentious works of Roman art in comparison with these...."

Pyramids of Geezeh from the Nile

Cairo: Bab Zuweyla - The bustling life near Bab el Mitwalli, today called Bab Zuweyla, the southernmost gate in the walls of the Fatimid city does not at all bring to mind a place of execution. And yet here in the heart of Old Cairo, from the Mameluke epoch onwards, capital sentences were carried out. The minarets which appear above the gateway are those of the Mu'ayyad Mosque, the Red Mosque, which flank the grand entrance on the outside.

Giza: the pyramids of Cheops and Chefren - *Vast constructions in an absolutely empty landscape from which man seems almost to be banished, but by which he is also fascinated and attracted: the pyramid of Cheops stripped of its covering and without its point, that of Chephren, his son, the head of the Sphinx emerging out of the sand and the remains of other structures as far as the eye can see. All enveloped by the desert, and almost desert themselves.*

This is how the area of the pyramids appeared to travellers in in search of ancient ruins in Egypt last century: an arid realm of solitude in which the shade of a palm or a sycamore offered the only means of relief from the heat and fatigue.

Giza: the great Sphinx - *In his travel journal, Roberts admits to having been really struck by the dimensions of the pyramid of Cheops, or Great Pyramid, only when he started to climb it and that it was the Sphinx which aroused more powerful emotions in him.*

The enormous body buried in the sand waits once again, as it has had to wait many times before during its multi-millennial existence, to be dug clear in order to appear in its entirety to the eyes of men. Brought back to daylight already in the past by Amenhotep II and Tuthmosis IV, who under the Sphinx had dreams or visions which promised them sovreignty over the country if they freed it from the sand, it has suffered more than just the ravages of nature and the weather: the mutilated profile of the nose reminds us that the Sphinx was used as a target for the fire-arms of Mameluke soldiers during shooting practice.

Despite this, the sculpture continues to cast its mysterious spell. Even David Roberts, usually so precise in his drawings, seems not to have been immune to the enigmatic power to fascinate which emanates from that face, at least if we judge by the sketch in which a sand storm is about to break over the Sphinx and the groups of caravaneers who surround it: the positioning of the sun, Sphinx and pyramids is totally unreal, given the well-known fact that the Sphinx faces the East.

The necropolis of Beni Hasan - *The tombs of the Beni Hasan necropolis are cut in the rock face which runs along the right hand side of the Nile and were destined to hold the nomarchs of the Eleventh and Twelfth Dynasties. Several of them have characteristics which make them different from Egyptian building typology. The fluted columns tapering at the top, on which rests an abacus, as well as the decoration on the cornice above the architrave of the façade, call to mind the Doric style of the Greeks. Roberts notes that inside the tombs the walls are covered with the famous paintings showing the daily life and sports of ancient Egypt which were copied down by Champollion and others.*

Entrance to the Caves of Beni Hasan.

David Roberts R.A. L. Haghe.

Boat with slaves - *A boat glides over the calm waters of the Nile which seem to lap the pyramids of Dahshur, called the "Bent Pyramid" and the "Red Pyramid", and those of Saqqara; a boat like many others, but with a cargo of slaves.*
"...the slave boat (was)...owned by...a Greek who had the effrontery to tell me that he was a Christian...The trade must be profitable, since such a journey could be advantageously taken with eleven only of these poor wretches for the market...The Greek, in hopes of a customer, pointed out the best of them to me, and descanted on their points with the skill of a jockey. Some were modest and shy, others tittered and seemed much amused with my costume, a blouse and trousers not one-third the width of a Turk's. The best of these poor creatures was worth eighteen or twenty pounds sterling. I regreted that I had too few words of Arabic or Greek to tell the old rascal how much his occupation was abhorred in England."

Dendera: the Temple of Hathor - The Temple of Hathor at Dendera is one of the best preserved and dates back to the Ptolemaic era. The vestibule in front of it is made up of six rows of four columns, crowned with splendid capitals adorned with cow-eared heads of the goddess Hathor surmounted by sistra, an attribute of divinity. The magnificence of the work, the extraordinary richness of the sculptural and pictorial decorations and above all the colours, at that time still so vivid that they seemed to have only just been laid on, fascinated Roberts who noted that everywhere was literally covered with hieroglyphics from top to bottom and from one end of the ceiling to the other, inside and outside and right up to the narrow stairway where the light of day is unable to penetrate. The symbols, he wrote, went from a height of 15 feet to those of such minute dimensions that a magnifying glass would be necessary in order to examine them.

The work of digging the temple out of the sand had not yet been finished as we can see from the two drawings of the vestibule and that of one of the entrances to the sacred enclosure. Of the latter, only the upper part emerges, on which the sun's globe spreads its protective wings almost as if it wishes to extend its benevolence to the men who dawdle below.

Dendera Dec. 7th 1838

David Roberts R A

15

The Temple of Hathor and the "mammisi" - *Another drawing in which the vestibule of the Temple of Hathor appears on the left and on the right we can see the lateral colonnade of the "mammisi" from the Roman era.*

In the "mammisi" or "birth-house" ritual ceremonies connected with the birth of Ihy, the son of Hathor and of Horus of Edfou were celebrated.

The Temple of Month at Medamud - *Here we can only see five columns of the portico of the Temple of Medamud, which was built by Ptolemy VII Evergete II and was dedicated to the falcon-headed war god Month.*

The two central columns which flanked the portal are distinguished from the remaining three in that they have a composite capital instead of one with a closed lotus shape.

The ruins of Luxor - *The feluccas which glide silently on the Nile and the men near the "shadufs" for drawing water on both banks of the river seem unaware of the spectacular ruins of Luxor which along with the white minaret of the Abu el-Haggag mosque, stand out on the horizon.*

The sacred zone of Karnak - *The rosy dawn light strikingly highlights the distinct features of the various buildings in the great complex of Ammon at Karnak. From left to right we can see distinctly, the first pylon, the column of Taharqa and the second pylon, immediately followed by the columns of the immense hypostyle hall, the obelisk of Tuthmosis I and that of Hatshepsut. On the extreme right lie the columns and pillars of the Festival Hall of Tuthmosis III and the gateway of Nectanebo.*

The hypostyle hall at Karnak - Roberts was so over-awed when he saw the ruins of Karnak that he despaired of ever being able to express his feelings in his drawings. He wrote that it was so much more impressive than anything that he had seen up to that point that he was quite unable to paragon it with anything. He observed that a man looks like a pigmy next to the main columns which have a circumference of 35 feet, 6 inches and that the overturned blocks lying haphazardly around were so enormous that it was difficult to see how they could have been knocked down, let alone how it was ever possible to raise them.

Roberts, however, was right: even if his drawings, with the little groups of men which appear in them, are able to convey an idea of the proportions of the buildings at Karnak, they have not the power to convey to us the emotion felt by Roberts and whoever else has been there in person.

The three drawings reproduced here show us the forest of columns of the hypostyle hall, seen from various angulations. It is virtually impossible to find an undecorated square centimetre: the architraves, the capitals, shaped like open or closed lotuses, the shafts of the columns, all surfaces are covered with inscriptions and reliefs. The colours, although dimed by the passage of the centuries, still give substance to the images created by the ancient Egyptian artisans.

The column of Taharqa - *This column which stands all alone was part, with another nine columns, of the colonnade erected by Pharoah Taharqa of the XXVth Dynasty. In the background, the great hypostyle hall and the ruins of the second pylon can be partially seen. The hypostyle hall's impressive forest of columns, which seems almost like a petrified wood of papyri, made a profound impression on Roberts who made numerous drawings of it from various different angles.*

Karnak, the Nile and, on the other side of the river, the city of the dead - *The sun has just set behind the rise of the west bank of the Nile, where the pharoahs and princes of the New Kingdom hewed their tombs out of the rock hoping to save them from the sacrilegious avidity of robbers. Even in ancient times the royal tombs attracted numerous plunderers, despite divine malediction of whosoever dared to violate them. These plunderers tore the mummies to pieces in order to steal the precious jewelry which accompanied the dead in their journey into the next world. On this side of the river, suffused by the golden light of the sun stands the city of the living, the "Thebes of a hundred doors" sung of by Homer, where innumerable Pharoahs in the succession of dynasties competed to leave evidence of the power and riches attained by the Country of Two Lands. Here pylons were raised, temples built and obelisks and monuments erected to honour the Theban triad: the great Ammon, the invisible god, "king of kings", his consort Mut and his son Khonsu. The generations of men who built these marvels have vanished into nothing, the multitudes of priests who officiated in the temples have also disappeared, the merchants and boatmen who thronged the quays along the Nile are no longer there, but these solitary ruins are still able to transmit their message of power and glory to whoever approaches them.*

Luxor: the colossi of Ramesses II and the remaining obelisk - Roberts saw only one of the two obelisks in red granite which had originally been erected in front of the pylon constructed by Ramesses II. A few years before his journey in Egypt, the missing obelisk had been transported to Paris and set up in the present day Place de la Concorde (1835-36). Two colossal seated statues flank the entrance to the great court. They are still buried up to the chest and are, as Roberts notes, sadly disfigured as is everything within reach of a hammer.
The man who we see seated on a stool intent on drawing is David Roberts who sometimes liked to portray himself in his sketches.

The great pylon of Luxor - The great pylon, like the other ancient monuments of Luxor, is surrounded by the mud houses of the inhabitants of the place, the structure of which is reminiscent of that of the pyramids. The large quantity of reddish clay vases to be seen on the flat roofs of the houses are nothing but pigeon-cotes.
On the top of the obelisk a falcon appears to be waiting to swoop down on one of the many pigeons which fly to and from, from and to the vases in which they have built their nests.
On the left behind the pylon, on whose towers the Battle of Qadesh fought by Ramesses II against the Hittites is celebrated, emerges the summit of the minaret, which Roberts describes as being afflicted with all the pain in the world in order to rise to the height of the enormous pylon, whilst, he continues, the obelisk, carved out of a single block, vanishes above it like the work of a god.

Grand Entrance to the Temple of

The disfigured colossus of Ramesses II - *The colossal statue of Ramesses II emerges from the accumulation of sand and rubble deposited in the course of centuries. On the top of the terribly disfigured head rests the double crown of Upper and Lower Egypt.*

General view of Luxor - *Called simply Nut, "the City", by the Egyptians, the ancient Thebes included both Karnak and Luxor. The latter occupied the southernmost part and was also the setting for majestic temples.*
In succession along the east bank of the Nile stand the obelisk of Ramesses II, then the great pylon of entry to the temple, immediately followed by the white minaret of the mosque of Abu el-Haggag, a venerated Muslim saint; beyond the sails of the felucca in the foreground, the magnificent colonnade of Amenhotep III reveals itself, followed by the ruins of the court in front of the actual temple.
Among the mighty ruins, life continues: the wretched white houses of the inhabitants, made from Nile mud, crowd close to one another and craft of various types and sizes sail on the river.

The Ramesseum and the colossi of Memnon - *Opposite ancient Thebes, on the other bank of the Nile, lies the city of the dead. Here the Pharoahs raised their mortuary temples, and, on the other side of the hills, their tombs were dug. Here we can see four Osiris pillars from the mortuary temple of Ramesses II, the Ramesseum, also called the Memnonium. The pillars portray the Pharoah in the shape of the mummified god Osiris, the god of the dead and the after life. These statues of Amenhotep III, the colossi of Memnon, have been mute witnesses of the daily rising of the sun for more than three thousand years. Set there to guard his mortuary temple, they emerge from the waters of the annual inundation of the Nile.*

Deyr el Medeeneh, Thebes.   David Roberts R.A.   L. Haghe lith.

The Temples of Deir el - Medina and of Sethos I at Qurna - *A small group of people watch an artist at work with interest: maybe Roberts himself dressed "Turkish style" in conformity with the custom in Egypt last century. The scene is set inside the little temple that Ptolemy IV erected at Deir el-Medina, the village where the workers from the royal necropolis of Thebes lived.*

The ruins of the mortuary temple of Sethos I at Qurna were used by Roberts as the background for this group of people gathered round a water-pipe. The central seated figure is an officer of the Pacha and on his left is the Sheik of the village. The only woman present is wearing a long veil and characteristic face mask which conceals the whole face, leaving only the eyes uncovered.

The vestibule of the Temple of Esna - *The Ptolemaic Temple of Esna, of which all that remains is the vestibule with 24 columns, is much lower than ground level due to the stratification of debris. Last century one could only reach the hypostyle hall by going down a flight of steps. Dedicated to Khnum, the ram-headed god, it brings to mind, with its splendid composite capitals and its astronomical symbols, the vestibule of the temple of Dendera.*

The Temple of Horus at Edfou - The Temple of Horus at Edfou is positioned on land higher than that of the Nile valley and it was started by Ptolemy III Evergete I in 237 BC.
Although it was still semi-buried in the sand and had village huts nestling on its roof and in front of the pylon, it made a great impression on Roberts who noted in his journal that he found himself looking at the most beautiful temple of Egypt which, although not as big as that of Karnak and not so well preserved as that of Dendera, possessed all that one could desire.

The portico of the Temple of Edfou - *From the sand emerges the upper part of the majestic columns of the portico of the temple of Edfou. Magnificent capitals in different shaped pairs hold up the massive architrave with its carved decorations and its winged sun's globe, all of which serves as a base for the simple huts of the village. And yet nothing seems to detract from the beauty and dignity of this masterpiece.*

Edfou: the pylon and the portico - Once again we see the portico of the temple with the pylon (second in size only to the first pylon of Karnak) in the background. The extent to which the buildings are buried is such that several people have been able to comfortably install themselves on top of the columns of the portal leading into the hypostyle hall. Roberts wrote "Though half buried it is more beautiful than if laid open, and reminds me of Piranesi etchings of the Forum of Rome...". He went on to say that he was inclined to believe that if it was cleared, this temple would reveal itself as the most complete after that of Dendera.

The excavation work done by Mariette has shown that he was right.

The Nile at Gebel el-Silsila ... - *Shaduf at work and feluccas with sails unfurled to pick up the slightest breath of wind; in the background, the sandstone quarries. This is Gebel el-Silsila where the Nile flows through a narrow channel. For centuries the rock faces on both banks of the river were used as a source of material for the constructions of the New Kingdom Pharoahs.*
On the western bank, the outline of a strange mushroom-formed rock can be seen: the ancient quarrymen extracted the surrounding rock leaving it like that, a solitary witness of the labours of those who worked for the glory of the gods and of the Pharoahs.

... and at Aswan - *Another picture of the Nile, here at Aswan - in ancient times called Syene - with the island of Elephantine.
"We walked over the ruins of this ancient city, which crowns the height of a rock jutting out into the stream. Nothing remains but the brick walls; so, after making a drawing of this part of the river, we crossed over to the island of Elephanta, where we found no vestiges of its ancient temples save a few columns and masses of rubbish. I saw one solitary figure with the arms folded on the breast, holding flagellum and crook; and on examining the wall next the stream I found it composed of stone covered with hieroglyphics, which must formerly have belonged to a temple."*

The sanctuary of Kom Ombo - *The great temple of Kom Ombo, dedicated to the crocodile-headed god Sobk and the falcon-headed Haroeris, revealed very little of its original structure as a double temple before excavation in 1893. What was visible however - the bright colours of the decoration, the richness of the carving, the elegance of the capitals - was enough to dazzle visitors. It is assailed by the desert sands on one side and, on the other, the waters of the Nile, which have done much damage. This fascinating edifice among "a few houses peeping above the sand is all that can be now seen of the once proud Ombros. Like its rival, Dendera, it is now desolate."*

Phila., Nov.ʳ 18, 1838.

The island of Philae - *To travellers, drawn by its fame, and arriving there after having crossed endless burning expanses of sand and rock, the island of Philae must have seemed to be a real paradise. The boats were moored in a refreshing little bay, shaded by the green foliage of palms and sycamores and a little higher up were the pylons of the temple of Isis and the elegant Kiosk of Trajan.*

Philae had been a place of pilgrimage from ancient times because it was sacred to Isis, the consort of the good god Osiris who lay in eternal repose on the nearby island of Biga, access to which was prohibited to all human beings.

This drawing shows us the little island in all its loveliness, like a mirage of magical beauty in the desolate landscape which surrounds it.

In 1972-80, the entire complex of buildings, dating from the Ptolemaic era, was completely dismantled and accurately rebuilt on the nearby island of Agilkia, the conformation of which is similar to that of Philae, because of the construction of the High Dam on the Nile.

Philae: the Temple and the Kiosk of Trajan - *At the south end of the island, a vast court flanked with colonnades leads to the first pylon. Behind the central gateway we can glimpse the second pylon and on the extreme right appears the Kiosk of Trajan. This pavilion is one of the most beautiful monuments on Philae, despite the fact that its decoration was never completed. Of great elegance and harmony, it was reconstructed by the Emperor Trajan and has become the symbol of the island. It is made up of a single roofless rectangular room bounded by 14 columns, and the impression that it gave Roberts, as he records in his journal, was that the builders and sculptors had just left the site. He goes on to say that the sandstone is so light and the detail is so delicate and sharp that he found it difficult to grasp the fact that he was looking at a ruin two thousand years old.*

The Temple of Isis: the hypostyle hall - *In the small
hypostyle hall with eight pillars in front of the entrance portal to
the sanctuary of Isis, the colours of the paintings are still bright.
Roberts writes that he was amazed and enchanted by the elegance
of its proportions, but still more by the marvellous composition of
its colours which seemed to be only just laid on, and which, even
in the places where they had been exposed to sunlight, had
preserved their brightness.*
*On the ceiling, in a blue sky spangled with golden stars, we can
see the repeated figures of sacred beetle and vulture with wings
spread ; sacred boats "sail" on the structural elements of the
ceiling, under which the capitals bloom luxuriant; Pharoahs and
gods speak, by means of hieroglyphic inscriptions, from the
columns of the hall.*
*Not even the transformation of this hall in Coptic church in the
VIth century, at the time of Bishop Theodorus, was able to upset its
order or to impair its beauty: a few Greek crosses on the columns,
on a wall and on a broken altar is all that remains of the period in
which the Christian faith arrived here.*

A group of Nubians - A group of Nubians with their peculiar hair-style pose for their portrait. Of the arms they carry, only the spears are part of their normal weaponry, the swords and shields are intended for selling.

Abyssinian slaves and the Temple of Debod - A group of Abyssinian slaves, mostly women, on their way to the slave market of Cairo rest under the shelter of a stunted palm tree; one of them is preparing their meal based on durra, Indian corn. In the background the Temple of Debod can be seen. This temple was completely dismantled in 1960 and presented to Spain as a sign of gratitude for its contribution to the campaign to save the temples of Nubia.

The Temple of Kalabsha - *The mud houses of the village seem to press round the mighty walls of the Temple of Kalabsha, the ancient Talmis, for protection. This edifice is the largest temple in Nubia not hewed out of the rocks, and is dedicated to the Nubian sun god Marul, called Mandulis in Greek. It was built in the Ptolemaic era, on the site of an older building from the time of Amenhotep II, and later rebuilt and added to under Augustus. Roberts describes the approach to the temple as being a road of great square blocks which started at the river bank and led right up to a raised platform on to which the pylons flanking the great entrance faced.*

After the pylon, and beyond the court, in which the pillars that once surrounded it on three sides lie scattered, is the hypostyle hall, the façade of which has four columns still standing. Behind this lies the entrance to the sanctuary on top of which some huts can be seen.

In order to save it, the whole complex has been transferred to near the Aswan New Dam. Thus, unfortunately, it has lost its superb back-drop of harsh mountains towering behind it which rather than making it seem smaller, enhanced its grandeur.

Abu Simbel, as it was - *The most famous and impressive of the temples built by Ramesses II in Nubia are the rock ones of Abu Simbel on the West bank of the Nile. The smaller one is dedicated to his beautiful and very much loved wife Nefertari and the other is an astonishing glorification of Ramesses II himself. Never before had the wife of a Pharoah been portrayed on the façade of a temple with the same dimensions as the statues of her husband which flanked hers: an act of love on the part of Ramesses to the most loved of his wives, eternalised in stone in order that the memory of it would survive through the centuries.*

Abu Simbel: the temple -Robert describes this temple, brought to light by the indefatigable Belzoni as being the more remarkable, though virtually engulfed by the desert sand. The sight of a double row of colossal statues of the Pharoah greets the astonished visitor who enters the bowels of the mountain: these appear to hold up the ceiling of the hall which is decorated with carvings and paintings of the victorious enterprises of Ramesses II. At a distance of three thousand years from the undertaking which had seen the face and heart of the mountain moulded into images of the Pharoah and his wife, the same architectural

challenge presented itself once again. In a race against time whilst the water of the artificial lake rose much faster than expected, the two rock temples were cut into blocks and, with part of the surrounding rock, were transferred 90 metres higher and reassembled exactly as they had been originally. In February 1969 the "miracle of the sun" reoccured : its rays returned to pass through the whole length of the temple, penetrating the sanctuary and flooding the statues of Ammon, Harmakhis and the deified Pharoah with light. Only one statue remained untouched, that of Ptah, the god of darkness.

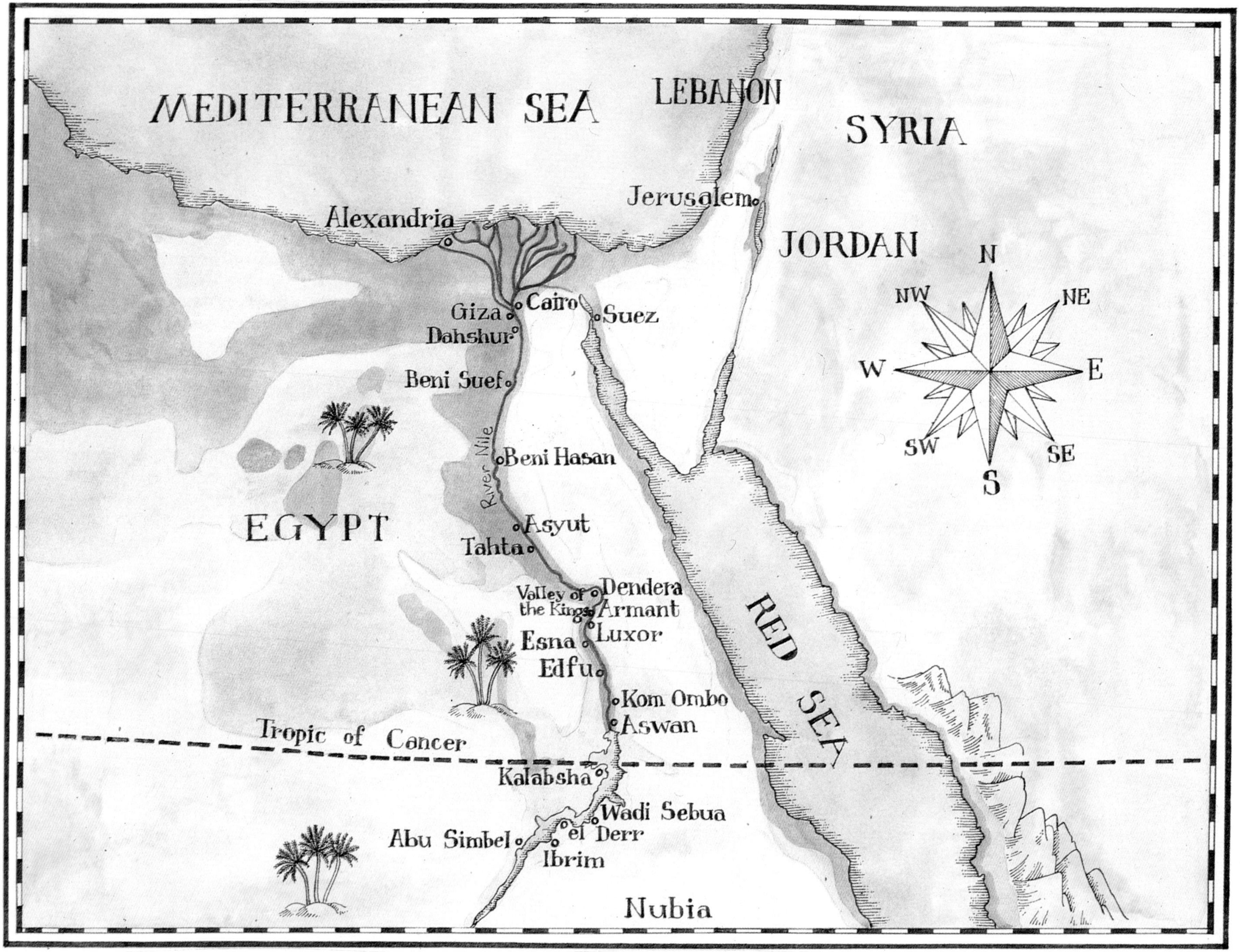
MEDITERRANEAN SEA
LEBANON
SYRIA
Jerusalem
JORDAN
Alexandria
N
NW
NE
W
E
SW
SE
S
Giza
Cairo
Suez
Dahshur
Beni Suef
River Nile
Beni Hasan
EGYPT
Asyut
Tahta
Valley of the Kings
Dendera
Armant
Luxor
Esna
Edfu
RED SEA
Kom Ombo
Aswan
Tropic of Cancer
Kalabsha
Wadi Sebua
el Derr
Abu Simbel
Ibrim
Nubia

A journey from Sinai
to the Holy Land

Introduction and commentary by Enrico Nistri

INTRODUCTION

When, on 11 September 1838, David Roberts boarded the steamship Dante and set off for the Near East, he left behind him an unhappy marriage and a fortunate artistic career that had begun only sixteen years earlier as a scene painter in a circus. His marriage with Margaret McLachlan, like himself a Scot, ran aground after only a few years. Roberts was left with one daughter, Christine; between one journey and another, he attempted to be a better father to her than he had been able to be husband to Margaret. His career, then newly consecrated by his election as Associate Member of the Royal Academy, was that of a "self-made man" of painting, of a self-taught artist who although he began at the very lowest step, as an apprentice house-painter, was able to demonstrate in only a very few years how a dearth of means and academic studies need not constitute an impediment to the emergence of true talent.

David Roberts, son of a family of humble craftsmen, was born on 24 October 1796 in the Edinburgh suburb of Stockbridge. His father was a cobbler; his mother, to whom he was deeply devoted, was the first to arouse his artistic sensibilities through her descriptions of the cathedral and convent of St. Andrew's, the city, once a bishop's see, in which she was born. And it was she who was at once the first victim and the privileged witness of the precocious artistic talent shown by her son, who covered the walls of her kitchen with chalk drawings of fantastic scenes inspired by circus posters and his curiosity about far-off places. Unable to pay the boy's way through school, his parents decided to send him, at the conclusion of his grade-school education, as apprentice to Gavin Beugo, a house-painter and decorator who after his own manner taught Roberts the technical rudiments of draftsmanship and drawing. At home, young David practiced painting on his own, demonstrating an extraordinary capacity for depicting real-life objects; for example, he once painted a copy of a one-pound note that was difficult to distinguish from the original!

When his apprenticeship came to an end in 1815, Roberts began working on his own as a decorator, specializing in imitation marble and wood; but very early on he began alternating this activity with that of theatrical scene-painter. His debut was of the most unpretentious, in a circus with a theater tent where, when the need arose, he was also called in play small parts. In return, as he travelled with his itinerant fellows-in-work, he was granted his first opportunity to give vent to his passion for seeing new places.

During a stop in York, he visited (and painted) the city's Gothic churches, thus confirming the lasting nature of that interest in medieval architecture that had been sparked by his mother's stories in boyhood.

The unassuming house-painter, whose imagination had been fired by the first plays he had seen from the gallery of the Edinburgh Theatre, and in particular by the exotic charm of an edition of Ali Baba and the Forty Thieves, would have seemed thus to have realized his most ambitious dreams. But in truth this was only the beginning of what was to be a brilliant career, which in 1819 took him to the Royal Theatre of Glasgow, the following year to the Edinburgh Theatre, and in 1822 to London, first to the Drury Lane Theatre and then, in 1826, to Covent Garden. Lauded by the critics (the Times defined him a genius of unusual talent), Roberts had also begun producing canvases; he exhibited for the first time in 1824 and was a founder of the Society of British Artists, of which he became president in 1831.

Artistic activity soon supplanted the scene-painter's craft, just as the latter had taken precedence over that of the decorator. But even as an artist, Roberts found ways to satisfy his innate wanderlust. He excelled as a painter of monuments, and in 1824 began a series of journeys, travelling in France, Belgium, Holland and Germany, where he produced sketches and paintings that were highly appreciated in that age before photography, when drawings and engravings were the tools for bringing far-off places into the homes of the public. In 1832-33 he spent eleven months touring Spain. After having visited Burgos, Madrid, Toledo, Cordova and Granada, he crossed the Strait of Gibraltar to Morocco, where he received his first taste of the oriental world and of Moorish architecture.

The journey, concluding with a lengthy sojourn in Seville, inspired a great number of oil paintings and drawings, of which many were published in the journal The Landscape Annual and many others in the volume entitled Picturesque Sketches of Spain. But above all, it assured Roberts' fame as an illustrator, and this enabled him to obtain the funding and support he needed for making his greatest dream come true: an expedition through Egypt and Palestine, which prepared with great care, weighing and uniting cultural considerations and practical necessities.

Roberts financed his travels with the profits from sales of his works on Spain, and counted heavily, for "marketing" his drawings and paintings, on the renewed interest expressed by Romantic Europe in exotic scenarios, on the re-discovery of Egyptian civilization following Champollion's unlocking of the theretofore unintelligible hieroglyphic code, on the eternal fascination exerted by the Holy Land and its monuments and that air of mystery that surrounded certain sites such as the fabulous Petra, the existence of which had been made known only very recently by an adventurous Swiss archaeologist. And for his journey Roberts was also able to count on the relative political stability of the area after Mehemet Ali, Pasha or Viceroy of Egypt, had extended his dominion to embrace the Holy Land and had initiated a process of modernization and assured conditions of greater tolerance toward Christian peoples.

Roberts sailed from Marseilles, whither he had arrived from Paris, and reached Alexandria - via Civitavecchia and Malta - on 24 September 1838. Together with a British couple, he rented a boat for three months to ascend the Nile - and was forced to literally "sink" it to free it from the rats with which it was infested. The boat, which cost the party fifteen pounds sterling per month, including the wages of the eight crew members, took the artist as far as Nubia and to the temples of Abu Simbel. There followed a long sojourn in Cairo, during which Roberts was the first Christian visitor to obtain permission to visit the mosques and to paint them. In the Egyptian capital he met John Pell and John G. Kinnear, two fellow British subjects, in whose company he decided to continue his trip to the Holy Land - or rather to Syria, as the entire area delimited by the Mediterranean Sea, the Euphrates, Asia Minor, the Arabian peninsula and Egypt was then called. The journey was conducted in conditions of extreme discomfort for a Westerner, and lasted from 7 February through 13 May 1839, when Roberts boarded ship for Alexandria, where he met Mehemet Ali.

Roberts landed in England on 21 July, with 272 drawings, a panorama of Cairo, three notebooks of sketches and a journal of his travels that his daughter Christine copied over and which is today preserved in the National Library of Scotland. In 1841, Roberts was elected Full Member of the Royal Academy. The exhibit of the watercolors and drawings he had made during his journey aroused enthusiastic commentary that pointed up the technical perfection and the skilful draftsmanship of the work: its

photographic accuracy, as we would say today. The Scottish Standard, for example, in a review of the Edinburgh show, observed how in not a one of the original drawings was "a blemish or slip of the pencil...
discernible. His touch seems magical." And the Spectator commented that "the artist has felt the sentiment of the scenes with the mind of a poet and depicted them with the accuracy of a draughtsman."

Immediately thereafter, on the tide of popular and critical success, commercial exploitation of the work began - although it was more to the benefit of the editor, Sir F. G. Moon, than the author. Moon, strong in the knowledge that he could count on a long list of subscribers, offered Roberts the sum of three thousand pounds sterling for the publishing rights in the drawings and their adaptation as lithographs by the Belgian engraver Louis Haghe. The amount, however conspicuous, repaid the artist only in part for the expense and danger of the journey - but in exchange, publication of the work assured Roberts' fame throughout Europe.

Egypt, Syria and the Holy Land, published in monthly installments from 1842 through 1849, made Roberts one of the most famous artists of the Victorian era. He was received at Court, was on excellent terms with many of the greatest artists and writers of the age, from Turner to Dickens and Thackeray, and boasted a clientele of wealthy businessmen as well as titled nobility and crowned heads. The former house-painter continued to travel, although all his later journeys were shorter and all within Europe. In 1843 he went to France, Belgium and Holland; in 1851 to northern Italy; two years later to Rome and Naples; and later again to Belgium and Paris. When he died, on 25 November 1864, the fame of this slow-speaking Scotsman with such a sure hand with a pencil, who generously aided novice artists and whom the Times considered "the best architectural painter that our country has yet produced," was still intact. The end of the Victorian era condemned Roberts, like many other protagonists of that era, to temporary oblivion. But today his paintings are again very much sought-after and his drawings have preserved intact the charm of a lost world, in which a journey through the Orient was still an adventure and such marvels as the temples of the Valley of Kings or the Holy Sepulchre were known to the public at large only through the mediation of art.

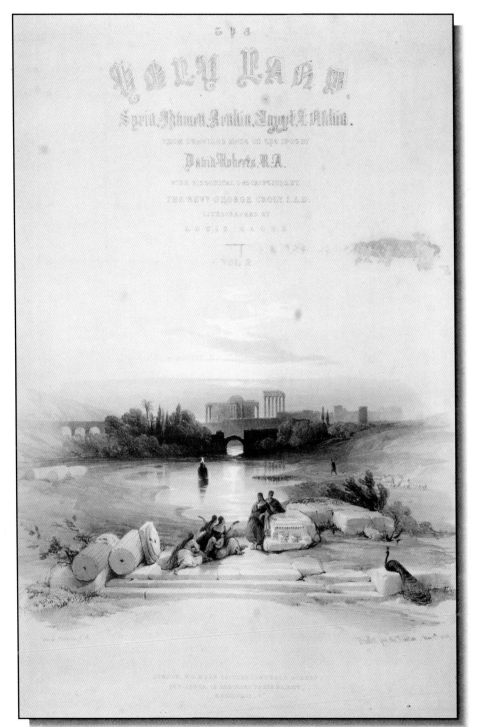

General View of Suez ...

David Roberts set out from Cairo for the Holy Land on 7 February 1839, with a small caravan including servants in Arabian and Turkish dress, an armed escort of Bedouins and twenty-one camels which transported provisions and baggage as well as tents for overnight encampments. With Roberts travelled two Englishmen, John Pell and John G. Kinnear, who two years later dedicated his own book of memoirs, Cairo, Petra and Damascus, to Roberts.

Guiding the party was Hanafi Ishmael Effendi (portrayed on the frontispiece), an Egyptian converted to Christianity during his stays in England, who spoke English fluently and with whom Roberts had become friends while in Cairo.

The first stop on their itinerary was the city of Suez, at the extreme southern tip of the isthmus of the same name, which had at the time yet to be cut through by Ferdinand Lesseps to place the Mediterranean in communication with the Red Sea.

... and a Scene on the Quay of Suez

The city of Suez, founded in the 15th century, had already gained considerable commercial importance as a stop-over for sailings to India and the East Indies. In his travel journal, Roberts described Suez as "a wretched place" and, even though he found the bazaars "picturesque", chose to depict in one of his drawings the quays of the port, somnolent by day but greatly animated by the arrival of the Bombay steamer during the night.

Suez at Suez. February 6th 1839.

DAVID ROBERTS R.A.

Ayn Mousa. The Wells of Moses

As tradition has it, the Ayn Mousa springs were made to appear by Moses in order to quench the thirst of the Israelites after their miraculous passage of the Red Sea. Yet today, the visitor coming from Suez follows a route analogous to that over which the Prophet led the Jewish people. Even though nearby there has since arisen Ras as-Suder, a small urban agglomerate established after oil was discovered in the area, the oasis itself has changed little since Roberts' arrival there on 12 February 1839. While the caravan halted for the mid-day meal, the artist counted fifteen springs "surrounded by a few stunted palm trees" and took time to paint a scene of the resting caravan.

Approach to Mount Sinai

The crossing of the Sinai Desert represented an adventure of no slight account for three European travellers who were completely ignorant of the desert routes and of the dangers they might encounter along the way. An armed escort of local Bedouins, like that shown in this drawing, was indispensible; one might say the necessary premise for a successful journey. Robert's journal entry dated 15 February notes with satisfaction: "We are now in the midst of the wilderness of Sinai ... we have now been nine days travelling this waste, and with the exception of meeting one or two Arabs of the same tribe, ... we seem as if cut off from the world ... I am every day more delighted with the manly intelligent countenance of our Bedowins."

An Ancient Egyptian Temple, on Gebel Garaba

At the end of a fatiguing climb on foot up a steep slope, Roberts and his travelling companions reached the ruins of Gebel Garaba, discovered by Niehbur in 1761. At the time, the ruins were thought by some to be the remains of a cemetery; by others, of a temple. Roberts and his fellow traveller Kinnear gave credit to the latter hypothesis, which has since been proved to be correct. The majority of archaeologists believe Gebel Garaba to be a temple dedicated to the Egyptian goddess Hathor, and due to its elevated position a place of pilgrimage. Hathor was known as "the Mistress of the Turquoise", a stone extracted in the area since the dawn of history.

Convent of Saint Catherine, Mount Sinai

The Convent of Saint Catherine was built in the sixth century by Emperor Justinian. The building, rising alongside the ancient hermits' tower and surrounded by walls, is considered to be the oldest continually-inhabited construction in the world. Tradition has it that the convent was built on the site of the Burning Bush seen by Moses; however that

may be, it stands at the feet of two mountains rich in sacred lore: Gebel Musa and Gebel Katerin. According to the Bible, it was the former mount that Moses ascended to receive the Ten Commandments; a holy legend dating to the eighth century narrates that the latter was the site of the deposition of the corpse of Saint Catherine after her martyrdom under Emperor Maxentius. The monastery library preserves rare manuscripts, among which the Codex Sinaiticus, *believed to be the oldest translation of the Bible.*

Principal Court of the Convent of Saint Catherine

Roberts, who in his journal described the convent as "a large square enclosure, the walls [of which] with flanking towers are built of hewn granite", was touched by the brotherly welcome he received from "our kind friends the monks of St. Catherine." On February

22, he noted in his journal how "it would be impossible to speak too highly of the attention and kindness with which we have been treated during our stay, particularly by the superior."

Little has changed in this monastic complex since the time of Roberts' journey: the most striking addition is the bell-tower, built in 1871.

Ascent to the Summit of Mount Sinai

The ascent of Mount Sinai was in olden times a compulsory penance for pilgrims, who in order to obtain forgiveness for their sins climbed the three thousand steps leading to the summit either on foot or on their knees, according to the gravity of their transgressions and the strength of their faith.

Although he took note of both the Hebrew and the Muslim traditions regarding the site, Roberts tackled the climb with the spirit of a layman. It took him about two hours; at the end of his labors, his strongest impression was of the beauty of the panorama that from the peak spread out below him. On 20 February he wrote in his journal, "Today we ascended to the summit of Sinai ... Near the top are two small chapels, one covers the cave where Elijah was fed by the ravens and the other is dedicated to Elias and on the summit are two others; one where Moses received the tables of the law and the other belongs to the Mahomedans; immediately under it is pointed out the footmark of the camel which carried him from Mount Ararat to Mecca. The view from the top is the most sublime that can be imagined."

61

The Rock of Moses ...

"Made a drawing of the rock of Moses said to be the same from which the waters gushed forth to the thirsty multitude," wrote Roberts in his journal for 22 February. The rock of Moses is a huge mass of red granite fifteen feet long, ten feet wide and twelve feet in height that is still today venerated by Christian pilgrims and Muslims alike.

... and the Encampment of the Oulad Said

This plate shows the arrival of the caravan in the encampment of the Oulad Said, friends of the Beni Said who escorted Roberts on his journey through the desert. The tribe was encamped in tents at the foot of Mount Serbal, a formation of red granite without a trace of vegetation. Roberts and his travelling companions were fascinated by the patriarchal welcome given them by the Arabs, who slaughtered a kid in their honor. Roberts' and his companions' trust in their hosts was bolstered by the fact that the Bedouins of the tribe had since time immemorial enjoyed the status of protectors of the Convent of Saint Catherine.

Fortress of Aqaba

Roberts reached the fortress of Aqaba, where he was received by the Governor, on the first of March. Situated at the extreme north end of the gulf of the same name on the Red Sea, the building as it stands today was built by the Egyptian Sultan Qansuh Ghoury in the 16th century on a square plan, with heavy towers at its corners. In Roberts' time it hosted a garrison of thirty; with its springs of pure drinking water, the fortress was also used as a storehouse providing supplies to pilgrims on the road to Mecca.

Sight of Petra, South

Inhabited since 7000 BC, Petra, which in the Biblical story was the land of Edom, saw the flowering of the civilization of the Nabateans, a nomadic people who first established camp there in the 7th century BC and exploited the strategic position of the site, a crossroads on the caravan routes along which were carried such goods as spices, silk and incense from China, India and Arabia. The Romans conquered Petra in 106 AD; the Arabs in the 7th century; the Christian Crusaders built a fortress in their turn. But the city was by that time already on the road to decline and its very existence was completely forgotten by the Europeans shortly afterwards. It was not until 1812 that the young Swiss explorer Johann Ludwig Burckhardt "discovered" Petra. On his travels through Jordan toward Cairo, Burckhardt, who knew the Arab language to perfection and even successfully masqueraded as a Muslim from India, heard many Arab legends about a hidden city in the impenetrable mountains, populated by Bedouins who were extremely distrustful of strangers. In order to gain access to the city without arousing undue diffidence, he expressed to his guide his desire to make a sacrifice at the tomb of the prophet Aaron - but upon his return to Europe he did not hesitate to make public his discovery of what has been called the rose-colored city of the desert.

Petra. Ancient Watch-Tower

After having spent some days in Aqaba, where he alternated drawing with finding solutions to the problems caused by his failure to receive his letter of introduction to the Sheik of the Alloweens, Roberts arrived in Petra on 6 March. One of the first sights that appeared before his eyes as he came upon the city was the ancient watch-tower with its two sole rooms, standing on a massive rock looming over the desert.

Petra. Ruins of a Triumphal Arch

When Roberts made his journey, the discovery of Petra was still a recent event, and - differently from today - it was an extremely difficult undertaking for a European to visit the city. In his journal, the artist described Petra as an "extraordinary city ... situated in the midst of mountains and ... abounding in every vegetable production." In order to enter it Roberts was forced, as visitors today still are, to ascend the Siq, the tortuous ravine cut by the Wadi Mousa torrent or perhaps opened by an earthquake, and to pass near the ruins of the triumphal arch erected in honor of the Emperor Hadrian on occasion of his visit to the city.

Petra. Views of the Eastern End of the Valley

A goodly number of the buildings in Petra are in truth great rupestrian sculptures. Since the era of the Nabateans, the particularly malleable rock of the surrounding mountains encouraged the inhabitants of the city to excavate rather than build up their temples and their homes. This architectural solution was simple only in appearance, however. Since the technique was such as to make it impossible to make major alterations as work progressed, the builders were forced to prepare detailed plans and to follow them closely.

The Palace Tomb shown in these drawings (which confirm Roberts' fame as the supreme "painter of architecture" of the English tradition) is perhaps the most monumental among Petra's rupestrian sculptures. The building, located in the area of the Royal Tombs, is laid out on three levels. While the lower one was entirely excavated into the living rock, the upper floors were in part built up using blocks of stone.

The particularly majestic appearance of the façade as seen from below relies on an optical effect that was carefully planned by the designer to increase the sense of perspective: each successive story was built to a lesser height than the one below it. Some archaeologists believe that the edifice was built during Roman times in imitation of Emperor Nero's Golden House.

The Theater, Petra

The theater of Petra, begun by the Nabateans in the 1st century AD but completed only by the Romans following the annexation of the kingdom to the Empire, is the only example of a Roman theatre entirely excavated into rock. The Latin architects had thirty-three hemicycles cut into the soft pink sandstone to give the complex a seating capacity of over seven thousand spectators. The building, "in a wonderful state of preservation," as Roberts' companion John G. Kinnear defined it in his own travel journal, was realized at the expense of pre-existing monuments, in most cases Nabatean tombs. The squared-off openings above the tiers of seats, clearly visible in the lithograph, are loculi that were re-opened with the precise aim of improving the acoustics of the theater and the rainwater drainage system.

Views of El-Khasne, Petra

Thanks to its position, El-Khasne Farun is one of the best-preserved buildings in Petra, as well as one of the most suggestive, especially in the early morning when the sun warms the pink of its sandstone. The edifice, rising as it does at the end of the Siq, almost as though it had been tucked away there to protect it from the weather, produces a dramatic effect on the visitor as it is suddenly revealed in all its splendor.

Its two floors are entirely sculpted into the rock face. The lower floor unites Nabatean motifs with elements taken from Classical architecture, such as the tympanum above the columns and the Corinthian capitals; at the center of the upper level is a circular templet, decorated with statues, with a conical roof. El Khasne Farun means "the Pharaoh's Treasury": the name can be traced to an ancient legend that relates how marauders hid a treasure there but then disputed its division in a battle with fire-arms. And the bullet holes still visible on the façade would seem to lend credence to the story.

Petra. El Deir

On 8 March, Roberts made what proved to be a tiring excursion to El Deir, a massive building dating to the Nabatean era. Its name means "the Monastery" in the Arab language; in Byzantine times it was used as a Christian place of worship, as is evidenced by the crosses carved in the walls. Inside the temple, which is entirely cut into the rock, the faithful gathered at the conclusion of ritual processions. The site offers a splendid panoramic view of the city and the royal tombs.

Ashdod

After leaving Petra, Roberts and his caravan reached Hebron on 16 March and then went on to Jaffa, where they arrived on 25 March after having seen Gaza, Askelon and Ashdod. The latter locality, ten miles out of Jaffa, appeared to Roberts to be "a small village with no remains". We read in his journal that the artist "passed Ashdod by moonlight" - but this fact did not hinder him from later painting a view of the city as it would have appeared in full daylight.

The locality is rich in Biblical lore: famous for its temple dedicated to the god Dagon, half man and half fish, Ashdod was at the center of the Philistine dominion and in perennial conflict with the Israelites. Conquered by Sargon in 710 BC, the city later fell under Greek rule and later still was annexed to the Roman Empire.

View of Jaffa from the South

Roberts liked Jaffa, surrounded by its magnificent orange groves and clinging to a hill overlooking the sea, as soon as he saw it. The city, which has today been encompassed by the modern Tel Aviv, capital of the State of Israel, is rich in Old and New Testament lore. According to the Hebrew tradition, Jaffa was founded by Noah's son Japhet; the town saw the prophet Jonah set sail for Tarsus and the shipping out to Jerusalem of the Lebanese cedar wood used in the construction of the Temple of Solomon. According to

the Acts of the Apostles, it was here that Saint Peter performed the miracle of the resurrection of Tabith and was inspired by God to receive the gentiles into the Church. During the age of the Crusades, Jaffa was fortified by Godfrey of Bouillon, who rebuilt the walls with the aid of Pisa; but the city fell under Muslim control in 1187 and remained thus through the time of Roberts' visit.
The plate shows in great detail the different architectural "strata" of the city, which amass Byzantine, medieval and Moorish elements. The figures in the foreground are Polish Jews, awaiting a boat on their return from a pilgrimage to Jerusalem.

Jerusalem. The Damascus Gate

Before setting foot inside the city of Jerusalem, Roberts made the circuit of the walls in the northwesterly direction, starting from the Damascus Gate, built in 1542 by Sultan Suleiman the Magnificent. Suleiman also raised the walls we see today on the remains of the ancient Roman circle, which in turn rested on the blocks of the rampart raised by Herod. The gate is still today one of the most picturesque and suggestive sights in the old city.
Of Jerusalem, in any case, Roberts was more impressed by the exterior than by the interior, more by the walls than by the streets. "The city within the walls," he wrote on 13 April, "may be called a desert, two-thirds of it being a mess of ruins and cornfields; the remaining third, with its bazaars and ruined mosques being of such a paltry and contemptible character that no artist could render them interesting."

The Pool of Bethesda

The Gospel according to Saint John relates that the Pool of Bethesda in Jerusalem, commonly called "the pool of probate", was the place where Christ performed the miracle of the healing of the lame man. It was actually made up of two large reservoirs surrounded by porticoes under which the blind, the lame and the paralytic sought refuge during the day. In 1839, as Roberts' drawing shows, the pool was reduced to a simple hollow containing a small lake of water. Excavations begun in 1871 by the architect Mauss brought to light the ruins of the original pools and the Sanctuary of the Lame Man built in early Christian times.

Following page:
Jerusalem from the Mount of Olives

Roberts had reached Jerusalem the night of 28 March, travelling from Jaffa through a countryside that seemed to him "carpeted with wildflowers" and "the most lovely I have ever beheld." Forced to make camp outside the walls of the city, the caravan was impressed by the perfect silence of the night, broken only "by the baying of a watch dog." The city that appeared to the artist from the Bethany road then counted about sixteen thousand inhabitants, among whom six thousand Jews, five thousand Muslim Arabs, three thousand Christian Arabs, and many pilgrims, mostly Greek and Armenian but also some Hungarians. The pestilence that had raged within the walls some months earlier did not dissuade Roberts from entering the holy city.

The Mosque of Omar

One of the most suggestive views of Jerusalem is that represented by the panorama of the vast man-made esplanade of al-Haram ash-Sharif ("noble sacred enclosure"), which contains sites and remains sacred to the three great monotheistic religions that lay claim to Jerusalem as their holy city. On the hill there once stood the Temple of Solomon, built by the wise Israelite king on the rock which according to tradition was the site of Abraham's sacrifice of Isaac. The Temple was demolished and rebuilt more than once before the destruction of Jerusalem in the year 70 AD and the Diaspora. After this date, in its place there remained only a large open ground, used as a waste dump and abhorred by the Christians, who saw in the ruin of the temple the confirmation of Jesus' prophecy reported in the Gospel according to Saint Matthew: "See you not all these things? verily I say unto you, There shall not be left here one stone upon another, that shall not be thrown down" (Matt. 24:2).

Following the Arab conquest, the Muslims venerated the rock, which had been sanctified by the presumed presence of Mohammed there, and built on it the imposing Mosque of Omar, also known as the Dome of the Rock (Qubbet as-Sakhra). The Crusaders, after their conquest of the holy city, transformed the mosque into a Christian temple; but following their rout the half-moon again returned to shine over Mount Moriah.

The Mosque of Omar, which appears clearly on the right, arises at the

center of a three-meter-high platform. Built in 691 by Byzantine artists, it is still, even in the wake of numerous restorations, one of the most suggestive monuments of Muslim art. The building is on an octagonal plan; at its center is set the dome with its cylindrical drum.

Originally erected in the eighth century, the mosque has been restructured many times and enlarged over the centuries; it seemed to Roberts "externally at least a tawdry piece of finery fast hastening to ruin." In truth, extensive restoration has been necessary, especially following the earthquakes of 1927 and 1937; it was performed by an Italian firm.

To the left of the mosque rises the Tower of Antonia; to its right is the white profile of the al-Aqsa (in Arabic, "far-off") Mosque, built on the site to which according to legend Mohammed was miraculously carried off from the Mecca.

The Exterior of the Holy Sepulchre and Calvary

The Basilica of the Holy Sepulchre is a maze of buildings overlaid the ones on the others through the centuries, comprising the Chapel of the Holy Sepulchre, Mount Calvary, the Chapel of the True Cross and various other chapels which recall episodes of the Passion of Christ. The history of the church coincides with the ups and downs in the history of Christianity in Jerusalem. Early on, with the intent of discouraging the practice of the Christian cult, Emperor Hadrian buried the entire area under the terraces of the Capitol of Aelia Capitolina. Following the Christian victory, Emperor Constantine's mother Helena had the first great basilica built on the site. It was destroyed by the Persians, partially reconstructed, and then again razed by the Arabs. The Crusaders rebuilt the structure seen by Roberts and which has remained intact down through our times.

Roberts depicted the south entrance to the basilica with its twin portals. One of these had been walled up since the time of Saladin, and guardianship of the other was and still is entrusted to two Muslim families. Until 1832, the Church had been opened only on occasion of great ceremonies and every pilgrim who entered was forced to pay a fee. Mehemet Ali, the Egyptian Pasha who occupied the Holy Land in 1831, finally abolished this tradition. But although access to the basilica had been liberalized, the tax on opening now fell to the three religious communities that provided services within it: the Catholics, the Armenians and the Greek Orthodox. During the Easter season (and it was during this season that Roberts was in Jerusalem), the courtyard in front of the entrance became a bazaar specializing in the sale of reproductions of sacred objects to the pilgrims - and this tradition continues even today.

Entrance to the Citadel

The Citadel of al-Qal'at rises near the Jaffa Gate; it is an irregular group of constructions built up over the course of the centuries and flanked by towers, among which there stands out to the northeast the so-called Tower of David. In 24 BC, Herod the Great built the Towers of Hippicus, Phasaël and Mariam within the area of the citadel to protect the northern portion of his palace. These constructions escaped destruction by Titus in 70 AD, but not at the hands of Hadrian, who sixty-five years later repressed the last of the attempts by the Jews to rebuild Jerusalem. The bases of the towers did, however, survive - and with their gigantic proportions enflamed the imaginations of the pilgrims, who believed them to be the work of King David. In Byzantine times, the Citadel offered refuge to the anchorites; the Crusaders, who re-baptized the Tower of David the "Castle of the Pisans" (Castrum Pisanorum), rebuilt the complex. It was destroyed anew in 1239, and finally rebuilt again in the 16th century in the form in which it was seen by Roberts.

Encampment of the Pilgrims at Jericho

At ten on the morning on April first, after having had some "considerable difficulty" in obtaining horses, Roberts left Jerusalem on a new itinerary through the most important sites in the Holy Land. His first stop was at the oasis of Jericho, to which he had been invited by the Governor of Jerusalem, Achmet Aga, who had also provided Roberts' escort. The locality, known to have been inhabited ten thousand years before Christ and rich in Biblical lore, was a delusion for the artist, who saw in Jericho only "a small tower around which were scattered a few miserable houses or sheds." The era of archaeological excavation which brought to light the various historical strata of the city, from the Bronze Age through the Crusades, had yet to begin. All in all, what struck Roberts most strongly was the oriental flavor of the encampment, with in the foreground the Governor's tent and the colorful costumes of the pilgrims from various countries.

Today, Jericho is a small city of about seven thousand inhabitants with modern buildings, elegant hotels and a pilgrims' hostel.

Descent to the Valley of the Jordan

Roberts sketched this view of the Jordan valley from the caravan track that from Jerusalem led to Jericho and from there to Mesopotamia and India. The artist was fascinated by the spectacle, which according to tradition coincides with the only sight of the Promised Land granted to Moses. Roberts confided to his journal that "The view, when we emerged from the rocky hills, was one not to be forgotten. The Valley of the Jordan lay stretched beneath our feet, in all the beauty of an Eastern evening. The Dead Sea, the silvery line of the rapid Jordan just visible, the gay colors of the pilgrim encampment glittering in the last rays of the setting sun, were fitter for the poet than the painter."

The Immersion of the Pilgrims

This drawing represents a scene common to many ancient pilgrimages to the Holy Land: bathing in the waters of the River Jordan at the place designated by tradition as that of Jesus' baptism. The origins of this pilgrimage date back to the first centuries of the Christian era, when in many cases the catechumens journeyed to the site in order to receive their baptism there. Even when during the period of Muslim rule bands of marauders tyrannized the area, persons intent on performing the ritual immersion at any cost often came to site in caravans of two to three thousand, escorted by armed troops.

Today, the Christians of Jerusalem make the pilgrimage on the occasion of the Epiphany; at the site of Jesus' baptism there now stands a chapel with a stair which permits descending to the water's edge and taking a boat across the river.

Banks of the Jordan. April 2nd 1839.

The Chapel of Saint Saba

Leaving the Jordan behind him, Roberts set out toward Bethlehem, and on his way saw the Valley of Fire over which looms the fortified convent of Saint Saba. He stopped there on the night of 4 April, receiving from the "friendly monks" of Greek Orthodox persuasion hospitality for his group and permission to make a sketch of the chapel dedicated to the saint. Rich in ornamentation, in the style typical of the Orthodox churches, the chapel pays honor to the saint born in 439 in Cappadocia, who at eight years of age withdrew from the world into hermitage in the desert. Shortly prior to Roberts' visit, in 1834, the 5th-century monastery had been damaged by an earthquake that had made restoration necessary.

Bethlehem. The Grotto of the Nativity

From the choir of the basilica, Roberts descended into the Grotto of the Nativity, the site attributed by tradition to the birth of Jesus. The grotto takes the form of a rectangle, about three and one-half meters wide by a little more than twelve in length. To the right as one enters are three lamps hanging over the manger in which the newborn Jesus was lain; on the opposite side an altar stands on the place the Wise Men supposedly laid down their gifts.
In Roberts' time, the grotto was illuminated by only fifty or so oil-burning lamps; today the walls are protected by a fireproof covering donated in 1874 by the then-President of France Mac-Mahon.

Bethlehem. Shrine of the Nativity

Having reached Bethlehem on the evening of 5 April, Roberts found accommodations with the monks of the Latin monastery and made a sketch of the interior of the Chapel of the Nativity, which stands on the traditional site of Jesus' birth. The cult of the sacred grotto is extremely ancient and has survived through the centuries despite the persecutions. Constantine and Saint Helena sponsored construction of a grandiose basilica, the original form of which was revealed by the excavations of 1934. The church we see today dates back to the time of Justinian and despite many modifications its structure has remained basically unaltered.
The church was spared by the Persian hordes that in 614 swept over Palestine: it is said that they were stopped by the sight of the portrayal of the three Wise Men in Persian national costume that adorns its façade.

81

Nablus

Following his visit to Bethlehem, Roberts returned to Jerusalem, where he stayed another week, from 8 through 15 April. The war that had broken out in Syria forced him to abandon his plans to travel to Damascus, but it did not hinder his continuing his journey through the south of Palestine and Lebanon. The first stop on his itinerary, on 17 April, was Nablus, the administrative center of Samaria, that Flavia Neapolis founded in the year 71 by Emperor Titus, who was probably reminded by the beauty of the area of the natural setting of Naples. Roberts liked Nablus too, and in his journal he defined it as being, with its gardens and abundant water, "by far the most beautiful town I have seen in Syria," Syria being in Roberts' time the appellative most generally used to indicate the entire Holy Land.

The drawing shows the minarets of the mosques of Jamia al-Kabir and an-Nasr, built using stones pillaged from medieval churches and Roman monuments in the nearby Sebaste; and the ancient synagogue of the Samaritans, where Roberts was allowed to view the manuscripts of the Samaritan Pentateuch. The synagogue was razed by the devastating earthquake that struck Nablus in 1927; today, the small surviving Samaritan community has moved out of the city to the foot of Mount Gerizim.

View of Nazareth

On 19 April, after one and one-half hours of travel up a winding trail, Roberts saw below him "the beautiful hamlet of Nazareth nestled as it were in the bosom of the hills by which it is surrounded." The city, which today counts almost forty thousand inhabitants, was at the time only a small group of houses encircling the monastery, founded in 1620, of the Franciscan fathers who extended their hospitality to Roberts. The locality, where the Archangel Gabriel appeared to Mary at the Annunciation and in which Jesus lived until his baptism, was a destination of pilgrimage as early as the time of Constantine.

Nazareth. The Fountain of the Virgin

"This fountain, with the groups of young women round it carrying their water jars was more suited for a picture than anything I have seen in the Holy Land," wrote Roberts, on 20 April, of the only fountain in Nazareth. It was here, according to one of the apocryphal Gospels, that the Virgin received the first visitation of the Archangel Gabriel as she drew water together with other young women her age. The fountain that is today shown to pilgrims - built in 1882 and restored in 1967 - does not stand on the exact spot as that which so fascinated Roberts.

Nazareth. The Church of the Annunciation

Since the earliest times of Christendom, Jesus' disciples and the descendants of the family of Mary venerated the place in which the Virgin lived and in which the miracle of the Annunciation took place. The first Western-style basilica was built here in the 5th century; on the remains of that monument, Tancred, as Prince of Galilee, ordered the construction of a sumptuous Romanesque church with a central nave and two aisles. When it was demolished in 1263 by the Turks, all that remained of the entire complex was the grotto bearing the still-legible inscription Verbum caro hic factum est *("Here the Word was made Flesh"). In 1730, the Franciscan fathers obtained official permission to build a new church; it is its interior that appears in Roberts' drawing. The building was enlarged in 1895 and then demolished in 1955 to make room for yet another new church, consecrated in 1969.*

Saint Jean d'Acre, from the Sea

Saint Jean d'Acre enchanted Roberts at first sight, when at about three in the afternoon on 23 April, coming from Tiberias, he caught his first glimpse of the city "with the blue Mediterranean." Its fortifications, which resisted even Napoleon Bonaparte, the fleet of warships arrayed offshore, the Carmel promontory ... all appeared, to his eyes, "a picture which would have satisfied Turner himself." Spoken of as Akko in the Bible, known later as Ptolemais at the time of the Maccabeans and later yet as Colonia Claudii Caesaris in honor of the Emperor Claudius, during the Crusades the city, today again known as Akko, took the name of Saint Jean d'Acre after the military order of Saint John. In Roberts' time, the memory of Napoleon's wounded soldiers, whom the Muslims had massacred in the Carmelite convent where they had sought refuge, had not yet faded, and the exploits of Ibrahim Pasha, who following a six-month siege succeeded in breaking down the city's resistance, were still recent history. In Roberts' view from the sea, we note the dome of the splendid al-Jazzar mosque, built on the model of Saint Sophia, and the fortified citadel which was later used as the central prison of the State of Israel.

Cape Blanco

Roberts arrived in Cape Blanco, one of the most suggestive natural beauty spots on the entire Syrian coast, on 25 April, in bad weather. This was an unfortunate circumstance for the traveller ("A heavy rain in the morning obliged us to wait until the middle of the day...") but favorable for the artist, who was thus able to depict Cape Blanco as a thunderstorm approached: "The sky was dark and louring; heavy clouds swept over our heads, and the rolling surge beat with a thundering noise on the rocks. It was certainly the most sublime scene I had yet beheld on the coast of Syria." Both the drawing and Roberts' observations in his journal concerning the scene testify to the sensitivity to the sublime in the natural world, typical of the Romantic age, of this self-taught artist who was very much in touch with the spirit of his times and anything but immune to its manifestations.

View of Sidon

Following a short stop in Tyre, Roberts proceeded to Sidon, where he stayed for two days, 27 and 28 April.
The ancient Phoenician city, first contemplated by the artist "from a little farmhouse with gardens of olive and mulberry trees", seemed to him to be "one of the finest I have ever seen in this country" and inspired many paintings. One of these is the view on the next page of the fortified Citadel, a construction probably dating back to Crusader times, which is linked to the mainland by a causeway bridge on four arches.

Baalbek. Remains of the Western Portico of the Temple of Jupiter ...

During his stay in the city, from 4 through 8 May, Roberts drew the magnificent remains of the temples of Baalbek from many different perspectives. This plate shows the Temple of Jupiter, the largest of all and built of a material similar to marble. Nine columns on the northern face, four on the southern face and six on the western side are the only ones still standing.

... and a Portion of the Eastern Portico

In this drawing, also inspired by a throughly Romantic attraction for the ancient ruins, depicts the remains of the Eastern Portico of the Temple of Jupiter. The fragments of columns, with their Corinthian capitals, strike the visitor's imagination for their grandeur in comparison with the the human figures and the massive majesty of the pillars.

Baalbek, General View

Once he had entered Lebanon and before heading south to Beirut, Roberts took a side trip to Baalbek, a city of ancient origin with superb ruins which had already attracted many European visitors. The Baalbek of old owed its importance to its position along the routes that linked Tyre and Palmyra. Some believe that the name Baalbek derives from

the ancient Semitic deity Baal; others that it is a corruption of the Hebrew word bekaa, meaning mulberry, a very common tree in the area. In the Hellenistic Age the city was re-named Heliopolis. The Romans held it in high esteem for its strategic position: during Augustus' rule they built a fortress and under Antoninius Pius, numerous grandiose temples. Under Constantine, the buildings were first abandoned and then converted into Christian churches before they finally fell into ruin following the Arab invasion.

Baalbek. The Circular Temple

Better preserved than that consecrated to Jupiter, the Circular Temple, although smaller than its imposing neighbor, was still larger than the Parthenon of Athens. It was originally conceived on two levels, both colonnaded; the lower order with Ionic capitals, the upper with Corinthian capitals. Visiting the ruins of this temple, and indeed those of all the monuments of Baalbek, was for a long time made impossible by the Lebanese Civil War.

Baalbek. From the Fountain

Touched by the poetry of the ruins, as were many other Western travellers of the age of Romanticism, Roberts confided to the page of his journal dated 4 May the feelings aroused in him during his stay in the Lebanese city: "Alas! what a change in all but nature herself - the fountain, the temple, the mosque are a mass of ruins overgrown with lichen and wild flowers through the midst of which the crystal stream still winds its way; but where are the gay citizens that once frequented its banks, where the maids who resorted here to make their offerings to its protecting deity, where the wealth and plenty that once belonged to this proud city?"

Although Roberts' exclamation might have a rhetorical sound to it and his prose is certainly less than original expression, his pictorial transpositions of his impressions, such as the romantic "landscape with ruins" reproduced here, are much more convincing.

Shortly after having completed this masterpiece, Roberts "took a last look of glorious Baalbek" and "took leave of Palestine." On 13 May 1839 he embarked at Beirut on the Magaria for Alexandria. He reached London "on 21st July, after having been eleven months absent."

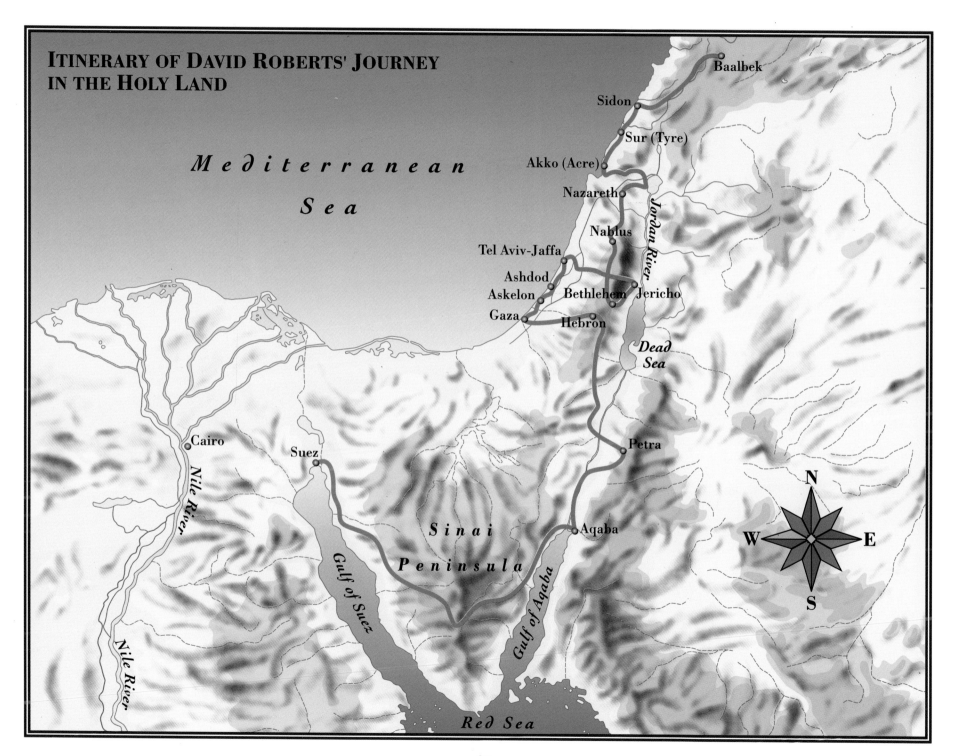

ITINERARY OF DAVID ROBERTS' JOURNEY
IN THE HOLY LAND

Mediterranean Sea

Baalbek

Sidon

Sur (Tyre)

Akko (Acre)

Nazareth

Jordan River

Nablus

Tel Aviv-Jaffa

Ashdod

Askelon

Bethlehem   Jericho

Gaza

Hebron

Dead Sea

Cairo

Suez

Petra

Nile River

Sinai Peninsula

Gulf of Suez

Aqaba

Gulf of Aqaba

Nile River

N

W   E

S

Red Sea

95

INDEX

Project and editorial conception: Casa Editrice Bonechi
Publication Manager: Serena de Leonardis
Graphic design: Serena de Leonardis
Picture research: Serena de Leonardis
Editing: Giovannella Masini
Make-up: Laura Settesoldi
Cover: Laura Settesoldi
Texts: Rita Bianucci and Enrico Nistri
Translation: Kate Parenti and Paula Boomsliter

Printed in Italy by Centro Stampa Editoriale Bonechi-Sesto Fiorentino.
Photographs from the archives of Casa Editrice Bonechi.

ISBN 978-88-476-2149-7

* * *